Did You Know?

WARWICKSHIRE

A MISCELLANY

Compiled by Julia Skinner

With particular reference to the work of Clive Hardy, Sarah Pernell, Julie Royle and Graham Sutherland.

THE FRANCIS FRITH COLLECTION

www.francisfrith.com

First published in the United Kingdom in 2010 by The Francis Frith Collection®

This edition published exclusively for Identity Books in 2011 ISBN 978-1-84589-531-0

British Library Cataloguing in Publication Data

Did You Know? Warwickshire - A Miscellany
Compiled by Julia Skinner
With particular reference to the work of Clive Hardy, Sarah Pernell, Julie Royle and Graham Sutherland.

The Francis Frith Collection
Oakley Business Park, Wylye Road,
Dinton, Wiltshire SP3 5EU
Tel: +44 (0) 1722 716 376
Email: info@francisfrith.co.uk
www.francisfrith.com

Printed and bound in Malaysia

Front Cover: **WARWICK, HIGH STREET 1922** 72343p

The colour-tinting is for illustrative purposes only, and is not intended to be historically accurate

AS WITH ANY HISTORICAL DATABASE, THE FRANCIS FRITH ARCHIVE IS CONSTANTLY BEING CORRECTED AND IMPROVED, AND THE PUBLISHERS WOULD WELCOME INFORMATION ON OMISSIONS OR INACCURACIES

CONTENTS

INTRODUCTION

Warwickshire is geographically 'the heart of England'. In 1974 under local government reorganisation a number of large metropolitan boroughs were formed, including the West Midlands, created by taking territory off Warwickshire and Staffordshire. This meant that Warwickshire lost its two great cathedral cities of Birmingham and Coventry, and with them its manufacturing and industrial heartland. With the decline of the Warwickshire coalfield the county was left with little in the way of industry, save for the manufacturing centres of Nuneaton and Rugby. Agriculture, however, remains important, as it always has been – many Warwickshire towns owed their early wealth to sheep and wool.

The heart of present-day Warwickshire is centred on Warwick itself, with Kenilworth, Leamington Spa and Stratford-upon-Avon all close by. In Kenilworth and Warwick are two of England's most famous castles: Kenilworth, a majestic ruin, and Warwick, a magnificent stately home. For centuries Warwickshire has been associated with some of the most famous names and events in English history: Henry II, King John, Richard Neville ('Warwick the Kingmaker'), John of Gaunt, Simon de Montfort, Henry VIII, Elizabeth I, Robert Dudley, Charles I, Oliver Cromwell, the Wars of the Roses, the English Civil War, and the Gunpowder Plot, to name but a few. But for many people today, Warwickshire is about Stratford-upon-Avon and William Shakespeare, who was born there in 1564 and retired home to Stratford at the end of his acting and playwriting career. Stratford is now the most visited literary shrine in the world, full of links with Shakespeare's life, works and family connections.

Traditionally, Warwickshire was divided into two areas: Feldon and Arden. The Feldon, south of the River Avon, was famous for its prosperous farms and charming villages, many with impressive 'wool churches' built with the wealth generated by sheep. North of the Avon, the Forest of Arden is hillier, with poorer soil, much of it wooded in former times although it was not a forest in the modern sense: the word 'forest' in the past meant any stretch of wild country, with woods and copses broken up by farms, villages, heaths and common land. The forest of Arden nowadays covers over 220 square miles, and around Henley and Tanworth there are places where the landscape is still recognisably that of the Arden that William Shakespeare knew.

BIDFORD-ON-AVON, BROOM 1910 62647

WARWICK, THE CASTLE, GUY'S AND CAESAR'S TOWERS 1892 31000a

WARWICKSHIRE DIALECT WORDS

'Batch' – a bread roll.

'Thrape' – to beat or thrash, as in ***'given a thraping'*** - given a beating.

'Gone out' – astonished, uncomprehending - ***'she looked at me gone out!'.***

'Kaggy handed' – left-handed.

'Donnies' – hands (especially of children).

'Waggin it' – playing truant, skiving.

'Nesh'– cold, as in ***'I'm neshed'*** - I'm freezing.

'Sneeped' – feeling small, belittled, slighted.

'Jizzup' – the gravy from a pie.

'Blarting' – crying.

'Mardy' – moody, miserable.

'The cut' – the canal.

EDGE HILL, THE CASTLE INN c1960 E102013

HAUNTED WARWICKSHIRE

It was near the Warwickshire village of Edge Hill in 1642 that the battle of Edgehill took place, the first major battle of the Civil War, and ghostly re-enactments of the battle are said to have been witnessed on many occasions ever since. In the 1740s a local squire built a folly in the village to mark the spot where the Royal Standard was raised (photograph E102013, page 7). The building became the Castle Inn during Queen Victoria's reign. Inside the inn is a collection of weapons found on the battlefield, and even a resident ghost – a spectral soldier from the battle is said to ride through the bar!

The White Swan Hotel at Henley-in-Arden is said to be haunted by the ghost of Virginia Black, a young lady of dubious virtue who died after falling downstairs after a quarrel with a client in 1845; her shade roams the corridor outside one of the bedrooms.

The legend of the 10th-century hero Guy of Warwick tells how he spent years killing dangerous animals and men to prove his love for Phyllis, daughter of the Earl of Warwick. He married Phyllis and became Earl of Warwick on the death of her father, but afterwards he went on a pilgrimage to the Holy Land. On his return to Warwick, full of remorse for all the deaths he had caused, he decided to live secretly as a hermit in a cave above the River Avon, near what is now the ruined Guy's Cliffe House. Phyllis found him as he lay dying, and nursed him until his death. Unable to live without him, she threw herself into the river and also died, and her distraught ghost haunts the area.

The historic Shrieves House Barn in Stratford-upon-Avon featured on Living TV's 'Most Haunted Live' programme. Paranormal investigations suggested that the building is haunted by up to 40 ghosts, one of which is its first owner, William Shrieve, but the most recently reported ghost is a small girl who moves the exhibits around at night.

Clopton Hall near Stratford-upon-Avon was the former home of the Clopton family. A local tradition says that one of the bedrooms is haunted by the ghost of Charlotte Clopton, who died during an outbreak of plague in 1564 and was buried in the vault of the Clopton chapel attached to Holy Trinity Church. Another member of the family died a short time after, but when his body was taken into the vault, Charlotte's body was found leaning against the wall: it appeared that she had not actually been dead when she was interred, and had woken from a coma to find herself buried alive. She had broken out of her coffin and had survived for a short while, but eventually died of hunger and despair, trying to claw her way out of the vault. Her ghost has haunted her family home ever since. Some people think this tale inspired the plot of Shakespeare's play 'Romeo and Juliet'.

The most famous ghost associated with Warwick Castle is the shade of Sir Fulke Greville, a former owner of the castle who was murdered in 1628 by his servant, Ralph Heywood, during an argument. Heywood struck at Greville with his dagger, then, horrified at what he had done, the servant killed himself by cutting his own throat. Greville, however, did not die instantly, but suffered a lingering death from his infected wound in his chambers in what is now known as the Ghost Tower. His ghost is said to emerge from his portrait and roam the castle grounds, groaning in agony.

WARWICKSHIRE MISCELLANY

In the Dark Ages, Warwickshire was part of the Anglo-Saxon kingdom of Mercia, whose most notable king was Offa, who ruled from AD757 to AD796, and for whom the village of Offchurch, near Leamington Spa, is named.

Warwick Castle is one of the most beautiful and best preserved castles in Britain. In 1268 it passed to the Beauchamp family, who set about its complete rebuilding. Its defences were formidable: in addition to the towers and curtain walls, it possessed a moat, drawbridge, barbican and portcullis, followed by a long passage to the inner courtyard. Attackers trying to get from the outer to the inner gateway faced a hazardous task.

Amongst the treasures in Warwick Castle are three portraits by Sir Anthony Van Dyck, the leading painter of Charles I's court, including his famous portrait of Charles I in armour, riding a white horse. There is also a macabre item on display in the Great Hall – a plaster cast of the death mask of Oliver Cromwell, who was the prime mover in the trial and execution of Charles I after the Civil War.

Warwick has comparatively few timber-framed buildings because a great fire destroyed much of the town in 1694, and it was subsequently rebuilt in brick and stone. St Mary's Church in Church Street was badly damaged in the fire, whose heat was so intense that it melted the church bells, but fortunately the interior survived. By 1704 a new nave and a Gothic tower had been built. One of the carillions of the church bells is 'Warwickshire Lads and Lassies', the regimental march of the Royal Warwickshire Regiment.

WARWICK, THE CASTLE ENTRANCE 1892 31007

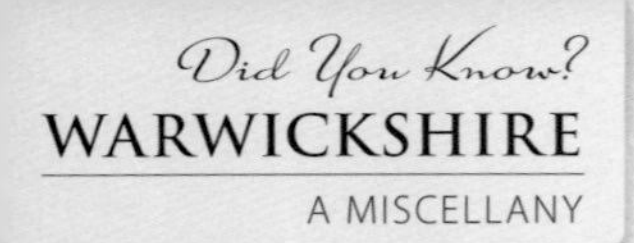

The only remaining parts of the medieval town walls which once surrounded Warwick are the east and west gatehouses. Photograph 72359 (below) shows the Westgate, which was once known as the hanging gate, as convicted felons were hanged here. Above the Westgate is St James's Chapel, which was renovated in the 19th century and contains work by William Morris, a leading member of the Arts and Crafts Movement.

The range of beautiful medieval buildings by the Westgate of Warwick seen in photograph 72359 (below) was originally the Guild House of St George and the Blessed Virgin. In 1571 Robert Dudley, Earl of Leicester acquired the buildings and transformed them into a 'hospital' (almshouse) for 12 old and disabled 'brethren' – usually ex-servicemen; the Hospital still serves this function.

WARWICK, WESTGATE AND THE LORD LEYCESTER HOSPITAL 1922 72359

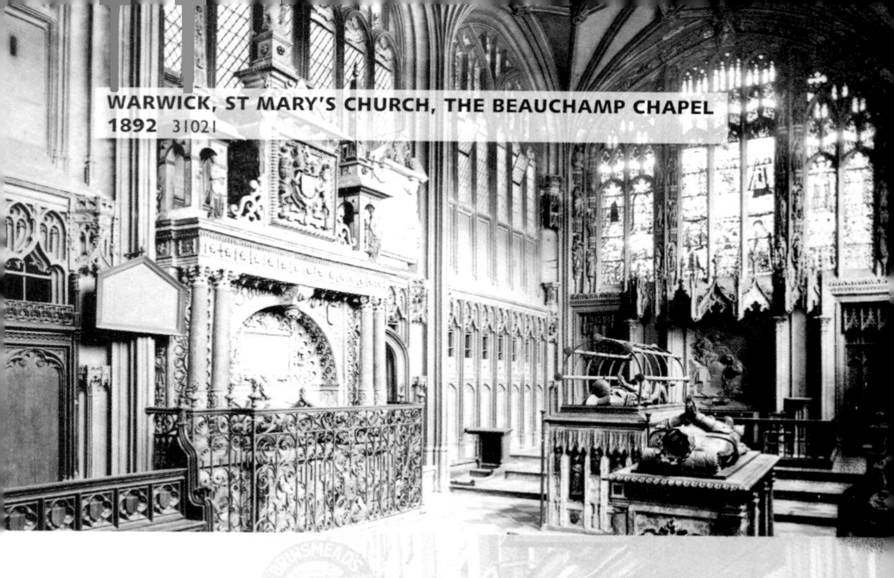

WARWICK, ST MARY'S CHURCH, THE BEAUCHAMP CHAPEL 1892 31021

St Mary's Church in Warwick contains the magnificent Beauchamp Chapel (photograph 31021, above). Its centrepiece is the tomb of Richard Beauchamp (1382-1439), 13th Earl of Warwick. The figure of the Earl lies under a cage-like structure, which at one time supported a velvet or brocade canopy. Also of interest is the monument to Thomas Beauchamp, 11th Earl of Warwick (1329-1369) and his wife, Katherine Mortimer. An unusual feature about their alabaster effigies is that the couple are shown holding hands. It is tempting to hope that this means they were an affectionate couple, but it is more likely that the monument symbolises the union of their two great houses when they married. Also in the chapel is the tomb of Robert Dudley, Earl of Leicester, who was a descendant of the Beauchamps and lived at nearby Kenilworth. The Earl's monument shows him clothed in armour and wearing a cloak. Beside him lies his third wife, Lettice Knollys, who died in her nineties; she was the granddaughter of Mary Boleyn, Anne Boleyn's sister. In the Great Hall of Warwick Castle is a tiny suit of armour which was made for Lettice and Robert's son, 'The Noble Imp', who died at a young age in 1584.

A link with Warwick's past is the annual Mop Fair in October, a reminder of the old Mop Hiring Fairs when people seeking employment came to Warwick to put themselves up for hire, carrying the tools of their trade; for example, a maid might carry a mop – hence the fair's name.

Beneath the courtrooms of the Shire Hall in Warwick is the old town dungeon, which could hold up to 50 prisoners. They were shackled to a chain which was connected to posts and than ran up the entrance steps to be secured at a point outside the door. You can still see the groove worn by the chain in the top step leading to the dungeon.

Some of the earliest English maps to show roads were actually made as a set of tapestries; these were woven by Richard and Francis Hyckes in 1588 for Ralph Sheldon. The Warwickshire Sheldon Tapestry Map is one of the prized items in the collection of the Market Hall Museum in Warwick.

Leamington Spa was mentioned in the Domesday Book of 1086 as 'Lamintone', but later became known as Leamington Priors to avoid confusion with Leamington Hastings, also in Warwickshire. Its development as a spa began in the 1790s, when William Abbotts discovered a mineral spring on land in what is now Bath Street, and established the original baths with Benjamin Satchwell. Soon more springs were discovered and developed, attracting large numbers of visitors to 'take the waters'.

Jephson Gardens in Leamington Spa were acquired for the town by Dr Henry Jephson in 1846; he is commemorated by a statue in the temple in the gardens. Money towards the laying out of the gardens was donated by another Leamington doctor, Dr John Hitchman, who is commemorated by a memorial fountain in the gardens. The gardens were re-opened in 2003, following renovation, and were voted 'Best Park in Britain' by the Royal Horticultural Society in 2004. Over the years, many plants and trees in Jephson Gardens have been donated in someone's memory. One such commemorates a Leamington man, Henry Tandey VC DCM MM; he was the most highly decorated private of the First World War, and was awarded the Victoria Cross for conspicuous bravery at Marcoing in 1918.

During the Second World War many Belgian and Czechoslovakian soldiers and Polish airmen were based in Leamington Spa, including the men commemorated by the Czech Fountain in the Jephson Gardens. The fountain is shaped like a parachute, with the water forming its strings, and between each channel are the names of the members of the Czechoslovak Brigade who in 1942 parachuted into Prague and assassinated the Nazi Reichsprotektor, SS Obergruppenfuhrur Reinhard Heydrich, known as 'The Butcher of Prague'. After the assassination the men were found and killed. A Rose Garden near the fountain is dedicated to the memory of the villagers of Liddice and Lasaky who were massacred by the Nazis in retaliation for the operation, which was planned in the town.

There were various pump rooms and water sources in Leamington Spa, but the only one to survive is the Royal Baths and Pump Room, usually referred to as the Pump Rooms, which opened for business in 1814. In later years Turkish baths were added, and also public baths – as an 'extra', for the cost of one shilling the bath would be cleaned for you before use! In 1997 the Pump Rooms complex was closed, rebuilt and refurbished, and reopened as the Royal Baths and Pump Room; spa water can still be obtained here.

LEAMINGTON SPA, ROYAL PUMP ROOM AND PARISH CHURCH 1922 72442

TURKISH
BATHS

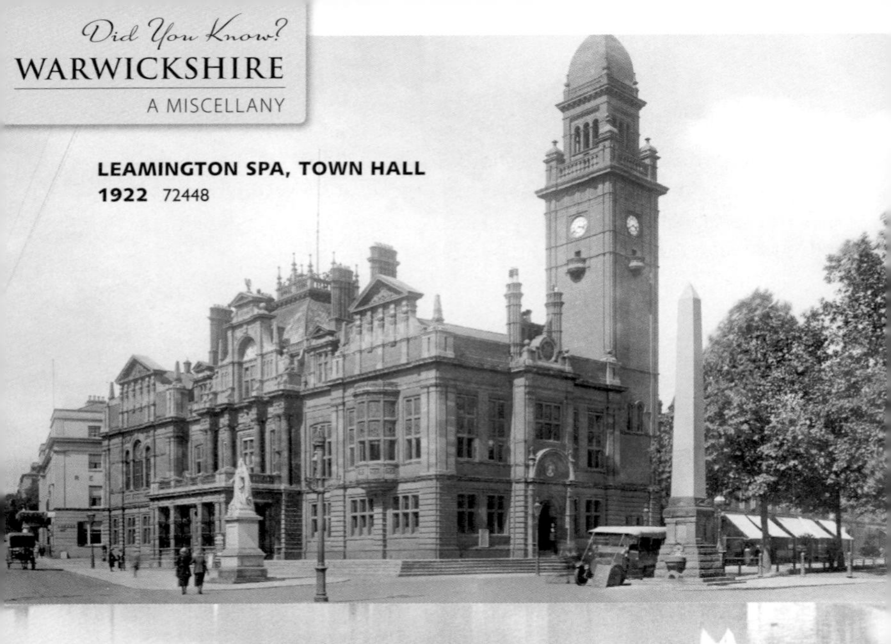

LEAMINGTON SPA, TOWN HALL
1922 72448

Leamington Spa's Town Hall, seen in photograph 72448 (above), is built in the Renaissance style with a campanile. The building is now home to Warwick District Council. The statue of Queen Victoria was erected outside the Town Hall in 1902, commemorating her visit to the town in 1838 when she came to drink the waters. It was Queen Victoria who allowed the town to assume the name of Royal Leamington Spa. The obelisk in Leamington Spa, to the right of photograph 72448 (above), commemorates Alderman Henry Bright, who was instrumental in providing the town with fresh water obtained from boreholes tapping underground sources – previously the town's water had come from the river, and was unsafe. The inscription on the obelisk reads: 'Erected by public subscription to record the services of Alderman Henry Bright to whose untiring exertions this town is chiefly indebted for its supply of pure water'. Ironically, the water supply at its base has now been turned off.

CHARLECOTE, CHARLECOTE PARK, FROM UPPER GARDENS c1884 17112

Stratford-upon-Avon is famous for its connection with William Shakespeare, but also has a long and fascinating history. By the 14th century it was a prosperous market town noted for its annual Mop Fair, when workers hired out their services for the coming year. The Mop Fair still fills the streets each October, but now with stalls and sideshows. The town gained its borough charter in 1553, by which time it was a centre for the manufacture of gloves. Malting (preparing barley for brewing beer) was also one of the town's principal trades. After it was linked into the canal system in the late 18th century the town became an inland port, busy with boats carrying heavy industrial loads. The commercial trade has now gone, but the canals have a new life as part of the leisure industry and the canal basin is colourful with narrow boats as holidaymakers moor up for a visit to the town.

Rother Street in Stratford-upon-Avon is named after 'Rother', the Anglo-Saxon word for cattle, and this was where the cattle market used to be held. In 1927 a mural dating from the mid 16th-century was found in the 15th-century White Swan Hotel at the top of Rother Street; it depicts the story of 'Tobias and the Angel', which was popular in medieval times, and can be seen in one of the bars of the hotel.

Stratford-upon-Avon's affairs were dominated in medieval times by the Guild of the Holy Cross. The Guild's power was destroyed in 1547, disbanded by order of Henry VIII, and the town was placed under the control of a bailiff; one holder of this office was John Shakespeare, William's father. The Chapel of the Guild of the Holy Cross is one of the town's oldest buildings; it was founded in 1269, but was rebuilt in the late 15th century. (It is the building with the tower in photograph 31070a, below.) The stained-glass windows of the chapel depict many of the leading citizens of the town's past. Inside the chapel are the remains of a 'Doom Painting', a mural depicting Judgement Day. The fortunate, worthy souls are shown ascending to heaven, whilst the sinners are tormented by demons and cast into the flames of hell.

STRATFORD-UPON-AVON, GUILD CHAPEL AND GRAMMAR SCHOOL 1892 31070a

STRATFORD-UPON-AVON,
SHAKESPEARE'S BIRTHPLACE AFTER RESTORATION 1861 S21602

William Shakespeare was born in a house in Henley Street in Stratford-upon-Avon in 1564, where his father, John Shakespeare, was a glover and wool merchant. Now owned by the Shakespeare Birthplace Trust, the building has been restored in line with the earliest known illustration of it, and the west part of the house is furnished in a late 16th- to early 17th-century style appropriate to a well-off family. However, one thing missing is the muck heap that was outside the front door in William's time – his father was fined on a number of occasions for not having the evil-smelling mound cleared away.

The Guild Hall of the Guild of the Holy Cross at Stratford-upon-Avon is shown in photograph 31070a, opposite. The ground floor was the Guild Hall proper, and the upper floor was known as the Over Hall. The building was erected in 1416-18. The upper floor was first used as a grammar school in 1553; the young William Shakespeare was educated at this school in the mid 16th century, and was perhaps recalling his schooldays when he later wrote of 'the whining schoolboy, with his satchel, and shining morning face, creeping like a snail unwillingly to school'.

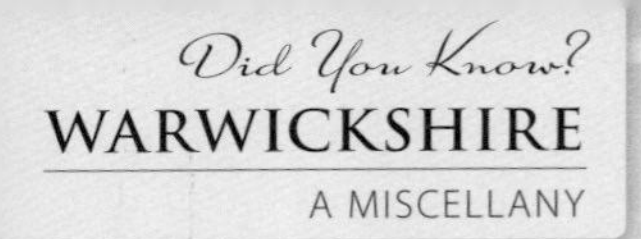

The village of Shottery near Stratford-upon-Avon is where William Shakespeare went to do his courting. His wife, Anne Hathaway, was the daughter of John Hathaway, a farmer. She was eight years older than William, who was eighteen when they married, and their daughter Susanna was born six months after the wedding. Anne's family home is shown in photograph S216118 (below); despite the name it is known by, it is not a cottage, but a spacious twelve-roomed Elizabethan farmhouse, and Anne Hathaway herself never owned it. Shakespeare's marriage to Anne produced three children, Susanna, born in 1583, and boy and girl twins, Hamnet and Judith, born in 1585. Susanna is buried inside Holy Trinity Church at Stratford-upon-Avon, close to her father, and Judith lies in the churchyard in an unmarked grave, but the location of the grave of Hamnet, who died at the age of 11, is unknown. Shakespeare appears to have been hit hard by his son's death: a quick-witted and charming young boy appears in many of his plays, and is believed by some scholars to be a commemoration of Hamnet Shakespeare by his father.

STRATFORD-UPON-AVON, ANNE HATHAWAY'S COTTAGE AT SHOTTERY c1965 S216118

Hall's Croft in Stratford-upon-Avon is a fine Tudor house that was the home of Shakespeare's eldest daughter Susanna, who married Dr John Hall. Hall's Croft is now owned by the Shakespeare Birthplace Trust, and contains a collection of fascinating items connected with 16th and 17th-century medicine.

The building in Stratford-upon-Avon's High Street which currently houses the Crabtree and Evelyn shop was once the town jail, with a cage on the outside of the building to hold prisoners. In later years it was the home of William Shakespeare's younger daughter, Judith. She married Thomas Quiney, a local wine merchant, and the building is now known as Judith Shakespeare's House, or, more correctly, Judith Quiney's House.

In 1597 William Shakespeare purchased a house in Church Street in Stratford-upon-Avon, known as New Place. He retired there, and it was where he died in 1616, leaving the house to his eldest daughter Susanna. New Place was demolished in 1759, but the site of the house forms part of the garden beside the splendid timber-framed Nash's House; this now houses the town museum but was once the home of Thomas Nash, who married Shakespeare's only surviving grandchild, Susanna's daughter Elizabeth Hall. The death of the childless Elizabeth in 1670 brought Shakespeare's direct line of descent to an end.

Holy Trinity Church at Stratford-upon-Avon is the burial place of Shakespeare, his wife Anne and other members of his family. The bust of Shakespeare in the church was placed there while his widow Anne was still alive, and she is believed to have confirmed that it is a good likeness of him. Nowadays entry to the actual church is free, but visitors are asked to pay a fee if they wish to visit Shakespeare's grave. His gravestone famously bears the words:

'Good frend for Jesus sake forbeare
To digg the dust encloased heare
Bleste be ye man yt spares thes stones
And curst be he yt moves my bones.'

Holy Trinity Church at Stratford-upon-Avon contains some fine examples of 15th-century woodcarving, stained-glass windows and several ornate tombs. One of the most interesting is that of Joyce Clopton and her husband, the Earl of Totnes. He was the Master of Ordnance to James I, and his office is reflected in the carvings on his tomb, which include representations of guns, cannonballs and barrels of gunpowder. The north door of the church is also notable for featuring a sanctuary knocker; any fugitives who reached it could claim temporary shelter in the church from their pursuers for 37 days.

Harvard House, on the right-hand side of photograph 72383 (below), is situated in the High Street of Stratford-upon-Avon, and was completed in 1596 for Thomas Rogers. His daughter Katherine married Robert Harvard in 1605, and it was their son John who was the main benefactor of Harvard University in the USA. An American bought this house in 1909 and gave it to Harvard University, which still owns it.

STRATFORD-UPON-AVON, HARVARD HOUSE 1922 72383

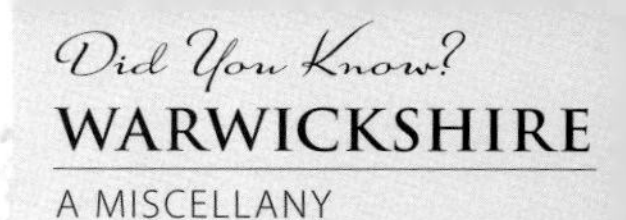

The statue of The Stratford Jester in Henley Street in Stratford-upon-Avon is by James Butler RA. The dancing jester holds a poll (a head on a stick) bearing the mask of comedy with his left hand, but his right hand, behind his back, conceals another poll with the mask of tragedy; the sculptor explained that it portrays the precarious balance of life: 'We dance through life finely balancing optimism above us, but tragedy lurks behind'. Quotations around the base of the statue are references to jesters and fools in Shakespeare's plays, including 'Foolery, sir, does walk about the orb like the sun; it shines everywhere' ('Twelfth Night'), and 'The fool doth think he is wise, but the wise man knows himself to be a fool' ('As You Like It').

Work on making the River Avon navigable from the Severn at Tewkesbury to Stratford-upon-Avon was completed in 1639. By the late 1780s the expanding canal network looked set to bypass Stratford-upon-Avon, and a canal was authorised by an Act of Parliament in 1793, to link up with the Worcester & Birmingham Canal at King's Norton. It did not open throughout until 1815, but this included a junction with the River Avon, which was navigable as far as Tewkesbury, where it joined the Severn.

The village of Claverdon in the former forest of Arden expanded greatly in the 1970s, but it is believed that the medieval village was enclosed within a deer park; a clue is the name of Park Farm, near the church of St Michael and All Angels. The church contains monuments to the Galton family of Edstone Hall, including Sir Francis Galton (1822-1911) who discovered that each individual has separate fingerprints.

BIDFORD-ON-AVON, THE OLD FALCON INN 1901 47340

Bidford-on-Avon is six miles from Stratford-upon-Avon. The 16th-century Falcon Inn at Bidford (photograph 47340, above) was once the scene of a drinking competition between the young William Shakespeare and his friends and a group of local lads known as the Bidford Sippers. The Stratford boys lost the bout and were too drunk to make the journey home, spending the night sleeping off the session under a crab-apple tree. The Falcon Inn has since been converted into private homes.

Henley-in-Arden was preceded by the settlement of Beaudesert, founded in the 11th century by Thurstan de Montfort who built a motte and bailey castle there. His descendant Peter de Montfort was involved in the Barons' War against Henry III, and after the king defeated the rebels at the battle of Evesham in 1265, the town of Beaudesert that grew up around the castle was destroyed. However, St Nicholas's Church at Beaudesert (built c1070) has survived, and Beaudesert is still a separate parish, distinct from Henley. The church's interior features a superb Norman chancel arch with elaborate carvings. The Norman south doorway also survives, with a zigzag-patterned arch.

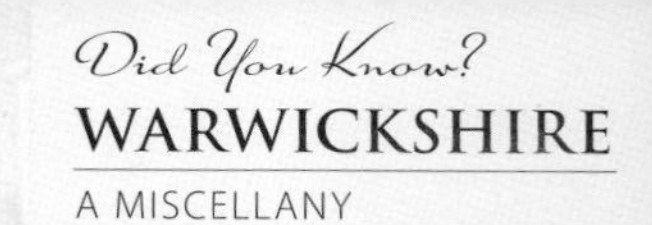

Henley-in-Arden is a fine example of a medieval settlement developing in linear fashion along a highway. The buildings that line the town's mile-long High Street span some seven or eight centuries, and display a glorious variety of architectural styles. The church of St John the Baptist was built c1450, and so was the timber-framed Guild House of The Guild of Holy Trinity, St John the Evangelist and St John the Baptist, seen in photograph H414022 (below). The Guild engaged in works of charity, but it was dissolved in 1547; the lower floor of its old Guild House is now in use as a public library.

HENLEY-IN-ARDEN, OLD GUILDHALL c1955 H414022

ALCESTER, HENLEY STREET AND TOWN HALL 1949 A113016

Alcester, eight miles west of Stratford-upon-Avon, was a staging post during the coaching era, but lost considerable trade when the railways replaced stagecoach travel. The town's principal industry in the past was the manufacture of needles. In the 16th century the area round the churchyard was the commercial centre of Alcester. This included Butter Street, so-named because it is a narrow street which receives little direct sunshine; this made it the ideal site for the sale of butter and other perishables in the past, as the shop premises would have been kept cool.

Alcester's picturesque Town Hall (in the centre of photograph A113016, above) was built as a market hall in 1618. It was purchased by public subscription in 1919 and dedicated to the memory of those who died in the First World War; it is officially now known as Alcester War Memorial Town Hall, but no longer has any municipal function.

The cottages at Wixford in photograph 47341 (below) have now been demolished, and a new house built on the site. However, St Milburga's Church is still there, and the churchyard contains a rare Grade II listed building, an 18th-century horse-house made of gorse and thatch, which was built to provide shelter for the mounts of visiting clergymen.

The name 'Napton' means 'settlement on the hill', so the suffix in the name of the eastern Warwickshire village of Napton-on-the-Hill is superfluous, although it does emphasise Napton's uniqueness as Warwickshire's only true hilltop village. Napton Hill is half-encircled by the Oxford Canal, which meets the Grand Union Canal (this stretch of which was formerly the Warwick and Napton Canal) at nearly Napton Junction.

WIXFORD, THE VILLAGE 1901 47341

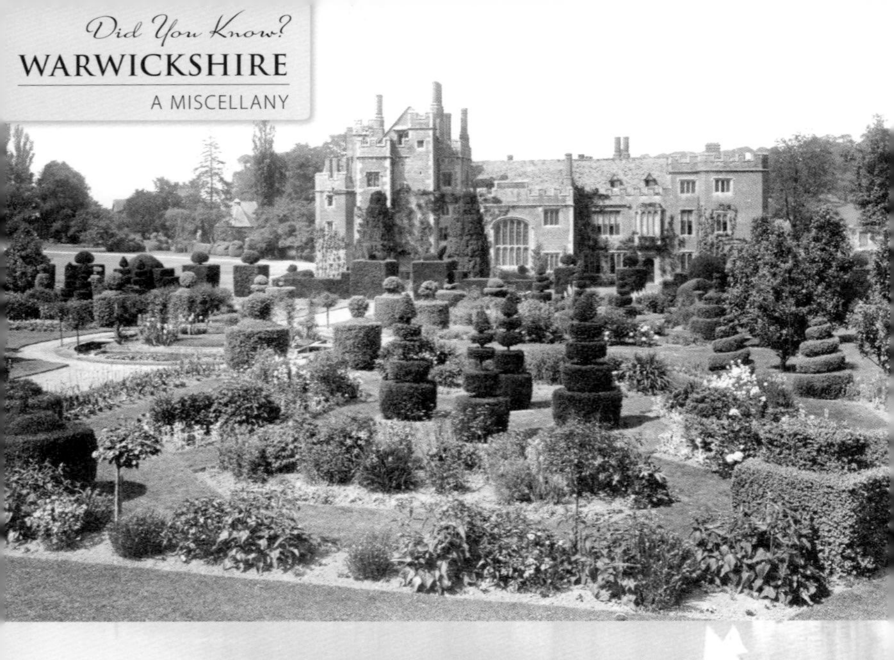

COMPTON WYNYATES, THE HOUSE AND THE GARDEN 1922 72098

Compton Wynyates was built between 1480 and 1520, and is one of the most beautiful houses in England (photograph 72098, above). In the late 18th century Compton Wynyates was abandoned by its cash-strapped owner, the 8th Earl of Northampton, and narrowly avoided being pulled down. In 1851 the 3rd Marquess of Northampton inherited the property and set about restoring it and remodelling the garden. In 1895 the 5th Marquess laid out the topiary garden, and a water garden was constructed on the site of the former moat. Compton Wynyates used to be called Compton-in-the-Hole, which refers to the house's idyllic setting in a hollow beneath Edge Hill.

For centuries Shipston-on-Stour, the 'Sheep town on the Stour', was a major sheep and wool market for the Vale of the Red Horse, a rural area of south Warwickshire named after the figure of a horse cut into the red clay which used to be visible on the hillside above the village of Tysoe. The figure, also known as the Red Horse of Tysoe, possibly dated from Saxon times, although it was first recorded in 1607. It was recut and reduced in size several times over the following centuries, but was finally covered over in 1910.

The town of Southam stands astride the Welsh Road formerly used by cattle drovers. According to local tradition, the 14th-century building in the town known as The Old Mint is so named because after the Civil War battle of Edgehill, in 1642, Charles I came here and demanded that the local gentry donate silverware to be melted down and minted into coins so he could pay his army.

Rugby lies on high table land in the Avon Valley, and its name may derive from the Celtic words 'droche', meaning 'rough' or 'wild', and 'brig', indicating a hilltop. Another ancient form, 'Rocheberie', has been interpreted as 'important place' ('roche') and 'stone' ('berie'), and this was the name by which the area was known in medieval times, changing to 'Rokeby' during the reign of Edward I.

Rugby's medieval market-place was situated at the intersection of ancient roadways linking Leicester to Oxford and Northampton to Coventry, and incorporated a 'shambles' where livestock were slaughtered and stalls set up for the sale of meat. By the 14th century the Shambles had become a row of shops with slaughtering yards behind, which were replaced in 1830 by a new row of shops known as Manor Buildings. By the 16th century, building had spread southwards from the Shambles, eventually forming the present High Street. The west side of Market Place was filled in during the 18th century to create Sheep Street on the east and Stockwell Lane, now Drury Lane, on the west. By the mid 19th century, in addition to a weekly market in Rugby there were 13 horse and cattle sales each year, plus a large Martinmas horse fair, 3 hiring fairs and 2 cheese fairs.

RUGBY, MARKET PLACE 1932 85177

BARCLAYS BANK
LIMITED
FRED BURN
Nº5
Nº5
DYERS
BARCLAYS
BANK
LIMITED
TC·1276

In medieval Rugby, scolds, troublemakers and women brewers who watered their ale were sent to the ducking stool at the Horsepool on the eastern side of the town, an area now known as The Plaisance.

Lawrence Sheriff, founder of Rugby School, was born in Rugby c1515. He spent the rest of his life in London, but in his will he left land and property for the foundation in Rugby of four almshouses and a school for boys. The influential Dr Thomas Arnold was Headmaster from 1828 to 1842, and under his guidance Rugby School became one of the country's leading public schools, with the emphasis on training character and producing 'Christian gentlemen' by encouraging religious and moral principles, gentlemanly conduct and intellectual ability. The author Thomas Hughes gave an account of Dr Arnold's headmastership in his novel 'Tom Brown's Schooldays', published in 1857.

RUGBY, CLOCK TOWER AND ST ANDREW'S CHURCH 1922 72125

Rugby celebrated Queen Victoria's Golden Jubilee in 1887 with the erection of the Jubilee Clock Tower in Market Place – shown in photograph 72125, opposite. The wooden building at the base of the clock tower in this view was a cabmen's shelter. Also in view is Rugby's parish church of St Andrew. Until the mid 19th century a curfew bell was rung from the church at 8 o'clock every evening, warning householders to extinguish their fires until morning – the original meaning of the word 'curfew', or 'couvre feu' in French, meant 'cover the fire', an attempt to reduce the risk of town fires in the past.

In 1857, Robert Stephenson, engineer of the London & Birmingham Railway, wrote: 'Few people have any notion how completely the whole system of our railways has been influenced by the bend northwards at Rugby'. When Stephenson chose to take his railway north of Rugby, the enforced sharp bend westwards towards Birmingham created a springboard for further lines to the north, turning Rugby into a major railway junction. Of Rugby's nine lines in 1900, five were closed by 1969, leaving two lines to London and those to Birmingham and Crewe. However, Rugby is now part of a direct line to Europe.

In 1925 the GPO erected 12 radio masts at the Imperial Radio Station at the Hillmorton area of Rugby, and the town's radio masts, later reduced to just four, are a well-known local landmark. The first transmitter sent messages for ships at sea and transmitted time signals sent from Greenwich. Today, the station transmits a precision time signal from an atomic clock. The second transmitter, opened in 1927, provided the first public telephone service to the USA, and was a forerunner of international communications.

The village green at Dunchurch near Rugby boasts a two-seater set of stocks, last used in 1866. Overlooking The Square in Dunchurch is Guy Fawkes House, a 16th-century building formerly the Lion Inn. On 6th November 1605, forty Catholic gentlemen met here to dine while they awaited news of the Gunpowder Plot to blow up the House of Lords during the State Opening of Parliament and assassinate James I. When they learned of the plot's failure they fled, but were later captured and executed.

Nuneaton derives its name from a priory for nuns founded in 1150. The town's first market was granted to the local prioress by Henry III, and there has been a market here for over 700 years; it still happens twice-weekly even now, with up to 115 stalls on a Wednesday, and over 200 on a Saturday. Among the market traders there in past times who used to draw the crowds was a man who sold foot oils and demonstrated the effectiveness of his product by jumping barefoot onto a wooden block studded with nails.

Riversley Park in Nuneaton was given to the people of the town in 1907 by Edward Melly, who was born in Liverpool in 1857, but came to Nuneaton after being educated at Rugby School. A mine owner, he was prominent in public life. The park was named after the Melly family home, which overlooked the River Mersey in Liverpool.

NUNEATON, MARKET PLACE c1945
N89010

NUNEATON, QUEEN'S ROAD c1945 N89017

The construction of the Coventry Canal in the late 18th century, and the fact that the coalfield town of Nuneaton later became a busy railway junction, made the town a busy manufacturing centre from the early 19th century onwards. There were coal mines, brick and tile manufacturers, iron works, worsted factories, ribbon makers and cotton and silk goods manufacturers to be found here.

One of the finest Gothic Revival houses in England is Arbury Hall near Nuneaton. The novelist George Eliot (real name Mary Anne Evans) was born in 1819 at South Farm on the Arbury Hall estate, where her father was the estate manager. Famous for such books as 'Middlemarch' and Adam Bede', she was one of the leading writers of the 19th century. Nuneaton's museum and art gallery holds a collection about her life and works.

Polesworth has developed beside the River Anker, with the original settlement on the north bank. Polesworth Abbey was founded by King Egbert in AD827, who installed his daughter (some say his sister) Editha as its first abbess. The present Abbey Church of St Editha dates from Norman times, and contains an effigy of an abbess dating from c1200; while this is too late to represent Editha, it is said to be the earliest effigy of an abbess in England. The 14th-century gatehouse shown in photograph 76124 (below) is also known as Nunnery Gate. Together with the oldest parts of the church, it is all that now remains of Polesworth Abbey.

Like the nearby village of Alvecote, Polesworth was once a mining area. Construction of the Coventry Canal began in the late 1760s, to link Coventry with the coalfield around Bedworth and open a navigation to the Grand Trunk (Trent & Mersey) Canal. The canal reached Atherstone in 1771, but then the finance ran out and it was not until 1790 that the canal reached a junction with the Frazeley & Birmingham Canal. Despite the delays in completing the cut, it was one of the most profitable of England's waterways, paying dividends up to 1947.

POLESWORTH, THE GATEHOUSE 1924 76124

MEREVALE, THE CHURCH FROM THE SOUTH 1924 76116

Only fragments of the Cistercian abbey founded at Merevale in 1148 survive, but a remaining building is the Church of Our Lady at Merevale, formerly the gatehouse chapel to the abbey which was used by visitors and servants. It is noted for its glass, including some probably paid for by Henry VII around 1500 in thanks for his victory over Richard III at the battle of Bosworth (1485), which was fought nearby. The traditional site of the battle is about eight miles from Merevale, but the historian Michael K Jones believes it was actually fought between Merevale and Atherstone; a contemporary source, the 'Croyland Chronicle', called it the battle of Merevale. Henry VII (then Henry of Lancaster, or Henry Tudor) stayed at Merevale Abbey the night before the battle, and later paid compensation for battle damage to the abbey and nearby villages.

ATHERSTONE, QUEEN ELIZABETH GRAMMAR SCHOOL c1955 A116007

The village of Atherstone is famous as one of only two places in England where the game of Shrovetide football is still played on Shrove Tuesday. The Atherstone Ball Game takes place along the public highway, a wild free-for-all with hundreds of people taking part, with no teams and no goals – the winner is the person who is able to hold on to the ball at the end of the game. The tradition celebrated its 800th anniversary in 1999, the game having been played in the village every year since the reign of King John.

SPORTING WARWICKSHIRE

Warwickshire County Cricket Club was formed in Leamington Spa in 1882, one of the 18 major county cricket clubs in England. The club is based at the county ground at Edgebaston in Birmingham, representing the historic county of Warwickshire as it was before local government reorganisation in the 1970s made Birmingham part of West Midlands. The name of its limited overs team (one day event) is the 'Warwickshire Bears', a reference to the bear on the Bear and Ragged Staff emblem of the Earl of Warwick in medieval times, and also on the Warwickshire County Council coat-of-arms.

Stratford-upon-Avon golf course was opened in 1928 by the famous Samuel Ryder, who is best known for donating the original Ryder Cup, which is contested by the USA and Great Britain. Samuel Ryder was captain of the golf club in 1929-30.

It was during a game of football in the Close at Rugby School in 1823 that the schoolboy William Webb Ellis first picked up the ball and ran with it. The sport (of rugby) that was born in that impulsive moment is now enjoyed worldwide, and the Close draws many visitors to see where it all began. In 1997 a statue of William Webb Ellis was unveiled by the rugby player Jeremy Guscott in front of the New Quad buildings of Rugby School.

Leamington Spa can claim to be the home of Lawn Tennis. Major Harry Gem, a local solicitor, founded the world's first club in the town. He and three friends set up courts just behind the former Manor House Hotel in 1872, and two years later founded a club. It was in Leamington Tennis Club that the modern rules of Lawn Tennis were drawn up in 1874. By 1884, the local press were carrying reports of tournaments in the town.

Warwick racecourse celebrated its 300th anniversary in 2007. The first race meeting took place in 1707, and Warwick Castle accounts record that £15 was donated by Lord Brooke 'towards making a horse race'. Early race meetings took place on St Mary's Common. Warwick was the first racecourse in Britain to include a race over obstacles, when a hurdle race was included as a novelty in 1831. The result is the earliest jump race result recorded in the Racing Calendar. The first stand at Warwick racecourse opened in 1809, and parts of this original stand still survive, making it one of the oldest in the country.

Warwick's football club is named Racing Club Warwick FC, because its ground is now next to Warwick racecourse. The club was founded in 1919 under the name of Saltisford Rovers, as games were then played on Saltisford Common, and changed to its present name in 1970. Racing Club Warwick FC won the Midland Football Combination championship in 1988 and the Polmac Services League Cup in the 2004/05 season. An England player who started his career at Racing Club Warwick FC was the goalkeeper Ben Foster, who played there in the 2000 season.

One of the most extraordinary sports stories associated with Leamington Spa is that of Randolph Turpin, who was born into one of the first black families to live in the town. A member of a boxing family, he was introduced to boxing in the local boys' clubs. He was immensely talented, and soon won the British middleweight title. This earned him the right to fight for the World title, and in 1951 he became World Champion, defeating the legendary Sugar Ray Robinson at Earls Court.

QUIZ QUESTIONS

Answers on page 52.

1. Which of William Shakespeare's plays was set in Warwickshire's Forest of Arden?

2. William Shakespeare died in Stratford-upon-Avon in 1616, aged 52. He left a strange bequest to his wife in his will, which has intrigued many people. What was it?

3. What is the link between Warwick and a famous name in theatrical history?

4. A plaque at a tree called the Midland Oak, at Lillington, north-east of Leamington Spa's town centre, is claimed to mark ... what?

5. What is the origin of the name of the little alley known as The Elephant Walk in Leamington Spa?

6. Which gruesome historical event was overseen by Richard Beauchamp, 13th Earl of Warwick, whose magnificent tomb is in St Mary's Church in Warwick? (The tomb is shown in photograph 31021, page 13.)

7. Which Warwickshire town features in Charles Dickens' novel 'Dombey and Son'?

8. George Plantagenet, Duke of Clarence (1449-1478) was responsible for the building of the Boar Tower and Clarence Tower of Warwick Castle before he joined the Earl of Warwick in rebellion against his brother, Edward IV. The rebellion was foiled, and the Duke of Clarence was put to death. He met his death in an unusual way – what was it?

9. The Shakespeare Monument in Stratford-upon-Avon, shown in photograph 72389 (below), was presented to the town in 1888 by the sculptor Lord Ronald Gower. Around the base of the statue are characters from the Bard's plays – who are they?

10. St Andrew's Church in Rugby was rebuilt between 1877 and 1885, and the east tower was added in 1895. However, the west tower is 14th-century, and is the oldest structure in Rugby. The church is shown in photograph 72125 on page 38, and is claimed to be the only church in the world to have... what?

STRATFORD-UPON-AVON, SHAKESPEARE'S MONUMENT 1922 72389

RECIPE

WARWICKSHIRE STEW

This dish is a way of cooking the tougher (and therefore cheaper) beef cuts very gently and slowly.

675g/1½ lbs stewing steak
2 tablespoonfuls seasoned plain flour
1 tablespoonful oil or beef dripping
150ml/5fl oz beef stock or red wine
6 potatoes, peeled and diced
4 carrots, diced
2 onions, cut into quarters
350g/12oz tomatoes
115g/4oz mushrooms, cut into quarters
2 cloves garlic, crushed
1 tablespoonful finely chopped fresh parsley
Salt and pepper

Pre-heat the oven to 140°C/275°F/Gas Mark 1.

Cut the beef into cubes, and lightly dust with seasoned flour. Heat the oil in a frying pan and fry the beef cubes in batches, to seal and colour the meat.

Remove the meat from the pan and place in a casserole dish, then add the stock or wine to the frying pan and heat gently, stirring all the time and making sure to scrape the bottom of the pan to collect all the flour.

Add all the remaining ingredients to the casserole dish and pour over the warmed stock or wine. Cover and cook for about 5-6 hours.

RECIPE

WARWICKSHIRE PUDDING

115g/4oz butter or margarine
75g/3oz caster sugar
3 eggs, beaten
225g/8oz plain flour
300ml/ ½ pint milk
350g/12oz raspberry jam

Cream the eggs and sugar together until light and fluffy. Gradually add the beaten eggs, a little at a time, adding a little flour if necessary to prevent curdling. Mix in the flour and milk, to make a batter.

Grease a 1.2 litre (2 pint) pudding basin, and line the base with 225g (8oz) of the jam. Pour in the batter. Cover the pudding basin with a lid of pleated greaseproof paper, and then another of foil, and tie down firmly with string. Place the pudding basin on a trivet or an upturned saucer in a large saucepan. Pour enough boiling water into the pan to come halfway up the sides of the basin. Place the pan on heat and bring the water back to the boil, then cover the pan with its lid and steam the pudding for about 1½ hours, replenishing the pan with more boiling water when necessary, so that it does not boil dry.

When the pudding is cooked, warm the remaining jam, turn out the pudding onto a warmed serving dish and serve with the warmed jam poured over the top.

QUIZ ANSWERS

WILLIAM SHAKESPEARE 1564-1616
S216162

1. Shakespeare's play 'As You Like It' was set in the Forest of Arden.

2. In his will, Shakespeare stipulated: 'I give unto my wife my second-best bed, with the furniture.' He left his best bed and most of his other property to his two daughters.

3. Sarah Siddons (1755-1831), who was formerly a housemaid at Guy's Cliffe House at Warwick, when her name was Sarah Kemble. Sarah eloped from Guy's Cliffe House one morning and married her sweetheart, William. She took to the stage and became the great actress Sarah Siddons, who was particularly famous for her portrayal of Lady Macbeth. In later years she became a welcome guest in the house where she had once been a maid.

4. The plaque marks the spot that is claimed to be the very centre of England.

5. In the 1800s Lockhart's Circus over-wintered in Leamington Spa. A reminder of those days is the name of The Elephant Walk, a narrow slipway to the River Leam just below the Mill Bridge Weir, where each day elephants from the circus were taken to drink, bathe and be scrubbed in the river.

6. Richard Beauchamp, 13th Earl of Warwick oversaw the trial and execution of Joan of Arc, who was burnt at the stake in France in 1430 during the Hundred Years' War.

7. Leamington Spa features in 'Dombey and Son' by Charles Dickens, where the town is the scene of Carker's first meeting with Edith Granger.

8. The Duke of Clarence ended his days in the Tower of London in 1478. Tradition says that as a favour from his brother, King Edward IV, he was allowed to choose the manner of his death, and he chose to be drowned in a butt of malmsey wine.

9. Prince Hal (later Henry V), who represents history; Falstaff, who represents comedy; Lady Macbeth, who represents tragedy; and Hamlet, who represents philosophy.

10. St Andrew's Church in Rugby is claimed to be the only church in the world to have two towers with ringing bells – the church has a peal of 5 bells in the medieval west tower and a second peal of bells in the Victorian east tower.

FRANCIS FRITH

PIONEER VICTORIAN PHOTOGRAPHER

Francis Frith, founder of the world-famous photographic archive, was a complex and multi-talented man. A devout Quaker and a highly successful Victorian businessman, he was philosophical by nature and pioneering in outlook. By 1855 he had already established a wholesale grocery business in Liverpool, and sold it for the astonishing sum of £200,000, which is the equivalent today of over £15,000,000. Now in his thirties, and captivated by the new science of photography, Frith set out on a series of pioneering journeys up the Nile and to the Near East.

INTRIGUE AND EXPLORATION

He was the first photographer to venture beyond the sixth cataract of the Nile. Africa was still the mysterious 'Dark Continent', and Stanley and Livingstone's historic meeting was a decade into the future. The conditions for picture taking confound belief. He laboured for hours in his wicker dark-room in the sweltering heat of the desert, while the volatile chemicals fizzed dangerously in their trays. Back in London he exhibited his photographs and was 'rapturously cheered' by members of the Royal Society. His reputation as a photographer was made overnight.

VENTURE OF A LIFE-TIME

By the 1870s the railways had threaded their way across the country, and Bank Holidays and half-day Saturdays had been made obligatory by Act of Parliament. All of a sudden the working man and his family were able to enjoy days out, take holidays, and see a little more of the world.

With typical business acumen, Francis Frith foresaw that these new tourists would enjoy having souvenirs to commemorate their days out. For the next thirty years he travelled the country by train and by pony and trap, producing fine photographs of seaside resorts and beauty spots that were keenly bought by millions of Victorians. These prints were painstakingly pasted into family albums and pored over during the dark nights of winter, rekindling precious memories of summer excursions. Frith's studio was soon supplying retail shops all over the country, and by 1890 F Frith & Co had become the greatest specialist photographic publishing company in the world, with over 2,000 sales outlets, and pioneered the picture postcard.

FRANCIS FRITH'S LEGACY

Francis Frith had died in 1898 at his villa in Cannes, his great project still growing. By 1970 the archive he created contained over a third of a million pictures showing 7,000 British towns and villages.

Frith's legacy to us today is of immense significance and value, for the magnificent archive of evocative photographs he created provides a unique record of change in the cities, towns and villages throughout Britain over a century and more. Frith and his fellow studio photographers revisited locations many times down the years to update their views, compiling for us an enthralling and colourful pageant of British life and character.

We are fortunate that Frith was dedicated to recording the minutiae of everyday life. For it is this sheer wealth of visual data, the painstaking chronicle of changes in dress, transport, street layouts, buildings, housing and landscape that captivates us so much today, offering us a powerful link with the past and with the lives of our ancestors.

Computers have now made it possible for Frith's many thousands of images to be accessed almost instantly. The archive offers every one of us an opportunity to examine the places where we and our families have lived and worked down the years. Its images, depicting our shared past, are now bringing pleasure and enlightenment to millions around the world a century and more after his death.

For further information visit: www.francisfrith.com

INTERIOR DECORATION

Frith's photographs can be seen framed and as giant wall murals in thousands of pubs, restaurants, hotels, banks, retail stores and other public buildings throughout Britain. These provide interesting and attractive décor, generating strong local interest and acting as a powerful reminder of gentler days in our increasingly busy and frenetic world.

FRITH PRODUCTS

All Frith photographs are available as prints and posters in a variety of different sizes and styles. In the UK we also offer a range of other gift and stationery products illustrated with Frith photographs, although many of these are not available for delivery outside the UK – see our web site for more information on the products available for delivery in your country.

THE INTERNET

Over 100,000 photographs of Britain can be viewed and purchased on the Frith web site. The web site also includes memories and reminiscences contributed by our customers, who have personal knowledge of localities and of the people and properties depicted in Frith photographs. If you wish to learn more about a specific town or village you may find these reminiscences fascinating to browse. Why not add your own comments if you think they would be of interest to others? See **www.francisfrith.com**

PLEASE HELP US BRING FRITH'S PHOTOGRAPHS TO LIFE

Our authors do their best to recount the history of the places they write about. They give insights into how particular towns and villages developed, they describe the architecture of streets and buildings, and they discuss the lives of famous people who lived there. But however knowledgeable our authors are, the story they tell is necessarily incomplete.

Frith's photographs are so much more than plain historical documents. They are living proofs of the flow of human life down the generations. They show real people at real moments in history; and each of those people is the son or daughter of someone, the brother or sister, aunt or uncle, grandfather or grandmother of someone else. All of them lived, worked and played in the streets depicted in Frith's photographs.

We would be grateful if you would give us your insights into the places shown in our photographs: the streets and buildings, the shops, businesses and industries. Post your memories of life in those streets on the Frith website: what it was like growing up there, who ran the local shop and what shopping was like years ago; if your workplace is shown tell us about your working day and what the building is used for now. Read other visitors' memories and reconnect with your shared local history and heritage. With your help more and more Frith photographs can be brought to life, and vital memories preserved for posterity, and for the benefit of historians in the future.

Wherever possible, we will try to include some of your comments in future editions of our books. Moreover, if you spot errors in dates, titles or other facts, please let us know, because our archive records are not always completely accurate—they rely on 140 years of human endeavour and hand-compiled records. You can email us using the contact form on the website.

Thank you!

For further information, trade, or author enquiries
please contact us at the address below:

The Francis Frith Collection, Oakley Business Park,
Wylye Road, Dinton, Wiltshire SP3 5EU.

Tel: +44 (0)1722 716 376 Fax: +44 (0)1722 716 881

e-mail: sales@francisfrith.co.uk **www.francisfrith.com**